To

_____

From

_____

OYEWOPO

50 Daily Faith Confessions for My Son

DOTUN OYEWOPO

50 Daily Faith Confessions for My Son

PUBLISHED IN AUSTRALIA BY
ACHIEVERS WORLD

50 Daily Faith Confessions for My Son
Copyright © 2020 by Dotun Oyewopo.
All rights reserved.

Requests for information should be addressed to:
dotunoyewopo@gmail.com

This book, or parts thereof, may not be reproduced, stored in a retrieval system, or transmitted in any form or by any means, electronic, mechanical, photocopying, recording or otherwise, without the written permission of the publisher.

ISBN 978-0-6489792-2-7 (paperback)

Printed in Australia

Every attempt has been made to credit the sources of copyrighted material used in this book. If any such acknowledgment has been inadvertently omitted or miscredited, receipt of such information would be appreciated

Unless otherwise noted, all scriptures are from *The Holy Bible, New International Version*. Copyright © 1973, 1978, 1984, 2011 by Biblica, Inc.® Used by permission of Zondervan. All rights reserved worldwide. www.Zondervan.com.

Scripture quotations marked (KJV) are taken from the *King James Version of the Bible*.

Scripture quotations marked (NLT) are from the *Holy Bible, New Living Translation*. Copyright © 1996, 2004, 2007 by Tyndale House Foundation. Used by permission of Tyndale House Publishers Inc., Carol Stream, Illinois 60188. All rights reserved.

Scripture quotations marked (GW) are taken from GOD'S WORD® Copyright© 1995 by God's Word to the Nations. All rights reserved

Scripture quotations marked (MSG) are taken from *The Message*. Copyright © 1993, 1994, 1995, 1996, 2000, 2001, 2002 by Eugene H.Peterson.

Scripture quotations marked (GNT) are taken from the Holy Bible, Good News Translation. Copyright © 1992 by American Bible Society.

Scripture quotations marked (ISV) are taken from the Holy Bible, International Standard Version. Copyright © 1995–2014 by ISV Foundation. All rights reserved internationally. Used by permission of Davidson Press, LLC. S

Scripture quotations marked (ESV) are taken from the Holy Bible, English Standard Version, copyright © 2001 by Crossway Bibles, a division of Good News Publishers. Used by permission. All rights reserved.

Scripture quotations marked (CEV) are taken from Holy Bible: Contemporary English Version. Copyright © 1995 American Bible Society.

Scripture quotations marked (NAS) are taken from the New American Standard Bible , copyright © 1960, 1962, 1963, 1968, 1971, 1972, 1973, 1975, 1977, 1995 by the Lockman Foundation. Used by permission.

Scripture quotations marked (CSB) from the Holy Bible, The Christian Standard Bible. Copyright © 2017 by Holman Bible Publishers. Used by permission. All rights reserved.

Words and phrases in Scripture quotations that are in **bold** or *italics* are the emphasis of the author.

Dedication

This book is dedicated to all parents who are ready to ground the foundation of their sons with faith confessions from their hearts.

This moment in your life is precious because God has destined that today, you will hold this book *50 Daily Faith Confessions for My Son*.

I believe and I am convinced beyond any doubt that God wants you to ask boldly for His blessings over your son. God has promised to answer all our requests if we ask Him in prayer.

"In that day you will no longer ask me anything. Very truly I tell you, my Father will give you whatever you ask in my name. Until now you have not asked for anything in my name. Ask and you will receive, and your joy will be complete"

(John 16:23-24, NIV).

Acknowledgment

I acknowledge the maker of heaven and the earth, the almighty God, the inspirational giver, the giver of visions and dreams. You are worthy of my praise. You gave me the book title, as well as wisdom and knowledge through the Holy Spirit. I couldn't have done it without you.

To my dearest husband, Oluwafemi Emmanuel Oyekunle Oyewopo, thank you for believing in me. You are my hero. You challenged me by setting the standard high. You gave me a push. Thank you for staying awake with me. I love you, my husband.

To my father-in-law and mother-in-law Daddy John Oyewopo and Mummy Deborah Oyewopo, you are the parents I have now. Thank you for your prayers and words of encouragement. Mummy Oyewopo, you are a great praying woman of God, and I am so grateful to you.

To my sons King David Boluwatife Abisoye Oyewopo and Father Abraham Adekolade Ayodeji Oyewopo, I am grateful to you both. I thank you for your encouragement and daily support. I am so proud to be called your mother.

To my precious siblings Pastor Adedoyin Osikoya, Adeleke Osikoya, Abolanle Idris, Taiwo Osikoya and Oluwafunmito Osikoya, I am very grateful to you all. Family is great; you are all great people in my life. Thank you all for our childhood. It is one beautiful memory I can never forget and will not trade for anything.

To all my spiritual fathers and mothers, thank you for your deposits of wisdom and grace in my life. Your teachings shaped my world view. You feed me with the eternal Word of God. Day and night, you all laboured with me. I am grateful to each of you.

To all my friends, thank you so much for your support and friendship, which I really appreciate. You have all been good role models to me. Your lives have challenged me.

To my brothers-in-law and sisters-in-law, I love you all and appreciate your prayers for me. Thank you so much.

"The tongue has the power of life and death, and those who love it will eat its fruit"

— (Proverbs 8:21, NIV)

CONTENTS

Power of Confession...1

Words of Life..3

Hear My Son..5

DAY 1...8

DAY 2...10

DAY 3...12

DAY 4...14

DAY 5...16

DAY 6...18

DAY 7...20

DAY 8...22

DAY 9...24

DAY 10...26

DAY 11...28

DAY 12...30

DAY 13...32

DAY 14...34

DAY 15...36

DAY 16...38

DAY 17...40

DAY 18...42

DAY 19	44
DAY 20	46
DAY 21	48
DAY 22	50
DAY 23	52
DAY 24	54
DAY 25	56
DAY 26	58
DAY 27	60
DAY 28	62
DAY 29	64
DAY 30	66
DAY 31	68
DAY 32	70
DAY 33	72
DAY 34	74
DAY 35	76
DAY 36	78
DAY 37	80
DAY 38	82
DAY 39	84
DAY 40	86
DAY 41	88

DAY 42	90
DAY 43	92
DAY 44	94
DAY 45	96
DAY 46	98
DAY 47	100
DAY 48	102
DAY 49	104
DAY 50	106
How to be saved	108

Power of Confession

Many believers do not understand confession — what it is and the power it has. Hence, we have not tapped into the full potential of our confessions. We have not seen or experienced the abundant promises of God in His Word.

Speaking the Word of God is completely different from confession. Therefore, it is important to understand the difference. Confession goes beyond simply speaking the Word. It is declaring what you are convinced of and hold to be true.

"The scripture says, 'I spoke because I believed.' In the same spirit of faith we also speak because we believe" (2 Corinthians 4:13, GNT).

With your heart you believe and with your mouth confession is made to righteousness. You must watch what you say because your confession either brings life or death. Our mouths are very powerful, so are the words that come out of them. The words we speak are alive and active.

"Watch your words and hold your tongue; you'll save yourself a lot of grief" (Proverbs 21:23, MSG).

"Words kill, words give life; they're either poison or fruit — you choose" (Proverbs 18:21, MSG).

"You are snared by the word of your mouth; you are taken by the words of your mouth"

(Proverbs 6:2, MSG).

"Let no corrupt communication proceed out of your mouth, but that which is good to the use of edifying, that it may minister grace unto the hearers" (Ephesians 4:29, KJV).

Words of Life

- You shall be the head and not the tail
- You are the first and not the last
- You are the victor and not the victim
- You are the winner and not the loser
- You are the accepted and not the rejected
- You are the light and not the darkness
- You are above and not beneath
- You are the master and not the slave
- You are the rising star and not the falling one
- You are the preferred and not the rejected
- You are the blessed and not the cursed
- You are healed and not the sick
- You are the rich and not the poor
- You are the redeemed and not the accused
- You are free and not the captive
- You are wise and not foolish

- You are a giant and not a dwarf

- You are a champion and not the defeated

- You are celebrated and not tolerated

- You are strong and not weak

- You are unique and not common

- You are mighty and not little

Hear My Son

"The eye that mocks a father and scorns to obey a mother will be picked out by the ravens of the valley and eaten by the vultures"

(Proverbs 30:17, ESV).

"Like a gold ring or an ornament of gold is a wise reprover to a listening ear"

(Proverbs 25:12, ESV).

"My son, give me your heart, and let your eyes observe my ways"

(Proverbs 23:26, ESV).

"The father of the righteous will greatly rejoice; he who fathers a wise son will be glad in him"

(Proverbs 23:24, ESV).

"Listen to your father who gave you life, and do not despise your mother when she is old"

(Proverbs 23:22, ESV).

"Hear, my son, and be wise, and direct your heart in the way"

(Proverbs 23:19, ESV).

"Train up a child in the way he should go; even when he is old he will not depart from it"

(Proverbs 22:6, ESV).

"Whoever spares the rod hates his son, but he who loves him is diligent to discipline him"

(Proverbs 13:24, ESV).

"The proverbs of Solomon. A wise son makes a glad father, but a foolish son is a sorrow to his mother"

(Proverbs 10:1, ESV).

"My son, keep your father's commandment, and forsake not your mother's teaching"

(Proverbs 6:20, ESV).

"Hear, my son, and accept my words, that the years of your life may be many"

(Proverbs 4:10, ESV).

"My son, do not despise the Lord's discipline or be weary of his reproof, for the Lord reproves him whom he loves, as a father the son in whom he delights"

(Proverbs 3:11-12, ESV).

"Trust in the Lord with all your heart, and do not lean on your own understanding. In all your ways acknowledge him, and he will make straight your paths"

(Proverbs 3:5-6, ESV).

"Making your ear attentive to wisdom and inclining your heart to understanding"

(Proverbs 2:2, ESV).

"But whoever listens to me will dwell secure and will be at ease, without dread of disaster"

(Proverbs 1:33, ESV).

"Hear, my son, your father's instruction, and forsake not your mother's teaching, for they are a graceful garland for your head and pendants for your neck"

(Proverbs 1:8-9, ESV).

"My son, if you receive my words and treasure up my commandments with you"

(Proverbs 2:1, ESV).

"My son, if your heart is wise, my heart too will be glad"

(Proverbs 23:15, ESV).

"Hear, my son, and accept my words, that the years of your life may be many"

(Proverbs 4:10, ESV).

Daily Faith Confession

DAY 1

Today, I confess that
God has made known the path of life to my son. He is coming
out of regret to joy.

"You make known to me the path of life; in your presence there is fullness of joy; at your right hand are pleasures forevermore"

(Psalm 16:11, ESV).

"A joyful heart is good medicine, but a crushed spirit dries up the bones"

(Proverbs 17:22, ESV).

Scriptural Meditation

Proverbs 17:22, ESV

Daily Faith Confession

DAY 2

Today, I confess that
my son is chosen and precious in the sight of God.
He is coming out of
rejection to acceptance.

"As you come to him, a living stone rejected by men but in the sight of God chosen and precious"

(1 Peter 2:4, **ESV**).

"But he said to me, "My grace is sufficient for you, for my power is made perfect in weakness." Therefore I will boast all the more gladly of my weaknesses, so that the power of Christ may rest upon me"

(2 Corinthians 12:9, **ESV**).

Scriptural Meditation

2 Corinthians 12:9, ESV

Daily Faith Confession

DAY 3

Today, I confess that God is with my son. He is coming out of pain to comfort.

"Blessed be the God and Father of our Lord Jesus Christ, the Father of mercies and God of all comfort, who comforts us in all our affliction, so that we may be able to comfort those who are in any affliction, with the comfort with which we ourselves are comforted by God"

(2 Corinthians 1:3-4, **ESV**).

"Even though I walk through the valley of the shadow of death, I will fear no evil, for you are with me; your rod and your staff, they comfort me"

(Psalm 23:4, **ESV**).

Scriptural Meditation

2 Corinthians 1:3-4, ESV

Daily Faith Confession

DAY 4

Today, I confess that
all will go well with my son, and he
will be in good health.
He is coming out
of sickness to health.

"You shall serve the Lord your God, and he will bless your bread and your water, and I will take sickness away from among you"

(Exodus 23:25, ESV).

"Beloved, I pray that all may go well with you and that you may be in good health, as it goes well with your soul"

(3 John 1:2, ESV).

Scriptural Meditation

3 John 1:2, ESV

Daily Faith Confession

DAY 5

Today, I confess that my son is free from the yoke of slavery. He is coming out of oppression to freedom.

"The Lord is a stronghold for the oppressed, a stronghold in times of trouble"

(Psalm 9:9, ESV).

"For freedom Christ has set us free; stand firm therefore, and do not submit again to a yoke of slavery"

(Galatians 5:1, ESV).

Scriptural Meditation

Galatians 5:1, ESV

Daily Faith Confession

DAY 6

Today, I confess that my son will not be put to shame. He is coming out of embarrassment to dignity.

"Fear not, for you will not be ashamed; be not confounded, for you will not be disgraced; for you will forget the shame of your youth, and the reproach of your widowhood you will remember no more"

(Isaiah 54:4, ESV).

"O my God, in you I trust; let me not be put to shame; let not my enemies exult over me. Indeed, none who wait for you shall be put to shame; they shall be ashamed who are wantonly treacherous"

(Psalm 25:2-3, ESV).

Scriptural Meditation

Daily Faith Confession

DAY 7

Today, I confess that God will open to my son His good treasury. My son is coming out of lack to superabundance.

"The Lord will open to you his good treasury, the heavens, to give the rain to your land in its season and to bless all the work of your hands. And you shall lend to many nations, but you shall not borrow"

(Deuteronomy 28:12, ESV).

"The Lord knows the days of the blameless, and their heritage will remain forever; they are not put to shame in evil times; in the days of famine they have abundance"

(Psalm 37:18-19, ESV).

Scriptural Meditation

Deuteronomy 28:12, ESV

Daily Faith Confession

DAY 8

Today, I confess that my son is coming out of hopelessness to expectation.

"As it is my eager expectation and hope that I will not be at all ashamed, but that with full courage now as always Christ will be honored in my body, whether by life or by death"

(Philippians 1:20, ESV).

"For surely there is an end; and thine expectation shall not be cut off"

(Proverbs 23:18).

Scriptural Meditation

Philippians 1:20, ESV

Daily Faith Confession

DAY 9

Today, I confess that my son is coming out of ignorance to wisdom and knowledge.

"If any of you lacks wisdom, let him ask God, who gives generously to all without reproach, and it will be given him"

(James 1:5, **ESV**).

"Beloved, do not believe every spirit, but test the spirits to see whether they are from God, for many false prophets have gone out into the world"

(1 John 4:1, **ESV**).

Scriptural Meditation

1 John 4:1, ESV

Daily Faith Confession

DAY 10

Today, I confess that my son is coming out of neglect to focus.

"Let your eyes look directly forward, and your gaze be straight before you"

(Proverbs 4:25, ESV).

"Fear not, for I am with you; be not dismayed, for I am your God; I will strengthen you, I will help you, I will uphold you with my righteous right hand"

(Isaiah 41:10, ESV).

Scriptural Meditation

Proverbs 4:25, ESV

Daily Faith Confession

DAY 11

Today, I confess that my son is coming out of opposition to acceptance.

"And call upon me in the day of trouble; I will deliver you, and you shall glorify me"

(Psalm 50:15, ESV).

"For the Lord has driven out before you great and strong nations. And as for you, no man has been able to stand before you to this day"

(Joshua 23:9, ESV).

Scriptural Meditation

Joshua 23:9, ESV

Daily Faith Confession

DAY 12

Today, I confess that my son is coming out of financial hardship to financial recovery.

"And rend your hearts and not your garments." Return to the Lord your God, for he is gracious and merciful, slow to anger, and abounding in steadfast love; and he relents over disaster"

(Joel 2:13, ESV).

"If you will remain in this land, then I will build you up and not pull you down; I will plant you, and not pluck you up; for I relent of the disaster that I did to you"

(Jeremiah 42:10).

Scriptural Meditation

(Joel 2:13, ESV).

Daily Faith Confession

DAY 13

Today, I confess that my son is born to be blessed and also be a blessing.

"And my God will supply every need of yours according to his riches in glory in Christ Jesus"

(Philippians 4:19, ESV).

"Every good gift and every perfect gift is from above, coming down from the Father of lights with whom there is no variation or shadow due to change"

(James 1:17, ESV).

"The Lord bless you and keep you; the Lord make his face to shine upon you and be gracious to you; the Lord lift up his countenance upon you and give you peace"

(Numbers 6:24-26, ESV).

Scriptural Meditation

Numbers 6:24-26, ESV

Daily Faith Confession

DAY 14

Today, I confess that my son is born to have a good life in Christ Jesus.

"Surely goodness and mercy shall follow me all the days of my life, and I shall dwell in the house of the Lord forever"

(Psalm 23:6, ESV).

"And you have made them a kingdom and priests to our God, and they shall reign on the earth"

(Revelation 5:10, ESV).

Scriptural Meditation

Psalm 23:6, ESV

Daily Faith Confession

DAY 15

Today, I confess that my son is born to inherit honour.

"For the sake of Jacob My servant, And Israel My chosen one, I have also called you by your name;
I have given you a title of honor. Though you have not known Me"

(Isaiah 45:4).

"You have made him for a little while lower than the angels; you have crowned him with glory and honor, and have appointed him over the works of Your hands"

(Hebrews 2:7).

Scriptural Meditation

Hebrews 2:7

Daily Faith Confession

DAY 16

Today, I confess that my son is born to gain wisdom.

"For the Lord gives wisdom; from his mouth come knowledge and understanding"

(Proverbs 2:6, ESV).

"The fear of the Lord is the beginning of wisdom; all those who practice it have a good understanding. His praise endures forever!"

(Psalm 111:10, ESV).

Scriptural Meditation

(Psalm 111:10, ESV).

Daily Faith Confession

DAY 17

Today, I confess that my son is born to gain foresight.

"Again Jesus spoke to them, saying, "I am the light of the world. Whoever follows me will not walk in darkness, but will have the light of life"

(John 8:12, ESV).

"Your eye is the lamp of your body. When your eye is healthy, your whole body is full of light, but when it is bad, your body is full of darkness. Therefore be careful lest the light in you be darkness"

(Luke 11:34-35, ESV).

Scriptural Meditation

(John 8:12, ESV).

Daily Faith Confession

DAY 18

Today, I confess that my son is born to gain revelation.

"But the wisdom from above is first pure, then peaceable, gentle, open to reason, full of mercy and good fruits, impartial and sincere"

(James 3:17, ESV).

"Who is wise and understanding among you? By his good conduct let him show his works in the meekness of wisdom"

(James 3:13, ESV).

Scriptural Meditation

James 3:13, ESV

Daily Faith Confession

DAY 19

Today, I confess that my son is born to gain insight.

"Whoever walks in integrity walks securely, but he who makes his ways crooked will be found out"

(Proverbs 10:9, ESV).

"I have counsel and sound wisdom; I have insight; I have strength"

(Proverbs 8:14, ESV).

Scriptural Meditation

(Proverbs 10:9, ESV).

Daily Faith Confession

DAY 20

Today, I confess that my son is born to occupy.

"I will restore the fortunes of My people Israel. They will rebuild and occupy ruined cities, plant vineyards and drink their wine, make gardens and eat their produce"

(Amos 9:14, HCSB).

"The Lord your God will drive them out from before you and remove them, so you can occupy their land as the Lord your God promised you"

(Joshua 23:5, NET).

Scriptural Meditation

Amos 9:14, HCSB

Daily Faith Confession

DAY 21

Today, I confess that my son is born to fulfil purpose.

"For we are his workmanship, created in Christ Jesus for good works, which God prepared beforehand, that we should walk in them"

(Ephesians 2:10, **ESV**).

"But you are a chosen race, a royal priesthood, a holy nation, a people for his own possession, that you may proclaim the excellencies of him who called you out of darkness into his marvelous light"

(1 Peter 2:9, **ESV**).

Scriptural Meditation

Ephesians 2:10, ESV

Daily Faith Confession

DAY 22

Today, I confess that my son is born to be celebrated.

"I am the one who gives them reason to celebrate. Complete prosperity is available both to those who are far away and those who are nearby," says the Lord, "and I will heal them"

(Isaiah 57:19, NET).

"The Lord is about to deliver me, and we will celebrate with music for the rest of our lives in the Lord's temple"

(Isaiah 38:20, NET).

Scriptural Meditation

Isaiah 38:20, NET

Daily Faith Confession

DAY 23

Today, I confess that my son is born to dominate.

"Far above all rule and authority and power and dominion, and above every name that is named, not only in this age but also in the one to come"

(Ephesians 1:21, ESV).

"For by grace you have been saved through faith. And this is not your own doing; it is the gift of God, not a result of works, so that no one may boast"

(Ephesians 2:8-9, ESV).

Scriptural Meditation

Ephesians 2:8-9, ESV

Daily Faith Confession

DAY 24

Today, I confess that my son is born to overcome. He will not be a victim of circumstances.

"And we know that for those who love God all things work together for good, for those who are called according to his purpose"

(Romans 8:28, ESV).

"I have said these things to you, that in me you may have peace. In the world you will have tribulation. But take heart; I have overcome the world"

(John 16:33, ESV).

Scriptural Meditation

Romans 8:28, ESV

Daily Faith Confession

DAY 25

Today, I confess that my son is born to multiply.

"He caused his people to multiply greatly; and be more numerous than their enemies"

(Psalm 105:24, ISV).

"He gives strength to the weary, And to him who has no might He increases power"

(Isaiah 40:29, AM).

Scriptural Meditation

Isaiah 40:29, AM

Daily Faith Confession

DAY 26

Today, I confess that my son is born to be fruitful. He shall eat the fruit of His labour.

"Whoever works his land will have plenty of bread, but he who follows worthless pursuits lacks sense"

(Proverbs 12:11, ESV).

"You shall eat the fruit of the labor of your hands; you shall be blessed, and it shall be well with you"

(Psalm 128:2, ESV).

Scriptural Meditation

(Proverbs 12:11, ESV).

Daily Faith Confession

DAY 27

Today, I confess that my son will not be intimidated by the Devil.

For God gave us a spirit not of fear but of power and love and self-control

(2 Timothy 1:7, ESV).

"Be strong and courageous. Do not fear or be in dread of them, for it is the Lord your God who goes with you. He will not leave you or forsake you"

(Deuteronomy 31:6, ESV).

Scriptural Meditation

Deuteronomy 31:6, ESV

Daily Faith Confession

DAY 28

Today, I confess that my son is the righteousness of God.

"God made the one who did not know sin to be sin for us, so that in him we would become the righteousness of God"

(2 Corinthians 5:21, NET).

"For our sake he made him to be sin who knew no sin, so that in him we might become the righteousness of God"

(2 Corinthians 5:21).

Scriptural Meditation

2 Corinthians 5:21

Daily Faith Confession

DAY 29

Today, I confess that my son is delivered from the power of darkness.

"And not frightened in anything by your opponents. This is a clear sign to them of their destruction, but of your salvation, and that from God"

(Philippians 1:28, ESV).

"He has delivered us from the domain of darkness and transferred us to the kingdom of his beloved Son"

(Colossians 1:13, ESV).

Scriptural Meditation

Colossians 1:13, ESV

Daily Faith Confession

DAY 30

Today, I confess that my son is redeemed by the blood of the Lamb.

"Indeed, under the law almost everything is purified with blood, and without the shedding of blood there is no forgiveness of sins"

(Hebrews 9:22, ESV).

"But God shows his love for us in that while we were still sinners, Christ died for us"

(Romans 5:8, ESV).

Scriptural Meditation

Hebrews 9:22, ESV

Daily Faith Confession

DAY 31

Today, I confess that my son is redeemed from the curse of the law.

"For the law of the Spirit of life has set you free in Christ Jesus from the law of sin and death"

(Romans 8:2, ESV).

"Christ redeemed us from the curse of the law by becoming a curse for us— for it is written, "Cursed is everyone who is hanged on a tree"

(Galatians 3:13, ESV).

Scriptural Meditation

Galatians 3:13, ESV

Daily Faith Confession

DAY 32

Today, I confess that my son is redeemed from sickness.

"Beloved, I pray that all may go well with you and that you may be in good health, as it goes well with your soul"

(3 John 1:2, ESV).

"The Lord sustains him on his sickbed; in his illness you restore him to full health"

(Psalm 41:3, ESV).

Scriptural Reflection

Psalm 41:3, ESV

Daily Faith Confession

DAY 33

Today, I confess that poverty has no hold on my son's destiny.

"For you know the grace of our Lord Jesus Christ, that though he was rich, yet for your sake he became poor, so that you by his poverty might become rich"

(2 Corinthians 8:9, ESV).

Have been young, and now am old, yet I have not seen the righteous forsaken or his children begging for bread"

(Psalm 37:25, ESV).

Scriptural Reflection

2 Corinthians 8:9, ESV

___
___
___
___
___
___
___
___
___
___
___
___
___
___
___
___
___
___
___
___

Daily Faith Confession

DAY 34

Today, I confess that doors of opportunities will be open for my son.

"And I will place on his shoulder the key of the house of David. He shall open, and none shall shut; and he shall shut, and none shall open"

(Isaiah 22:22, ESV).

"Ask, and it will be given to you; seek, and you will find; knock, and it will be opened to you. For everyone who asks receives, and the one who seeks finds, and to the one who knocks it will be opened"

(Matthew 7:7-8, ESV).

Scriptural Meditation

Matthew 7:7-8, ESV

Daily Faith Confession

DAY 35

Today, I confess that my son has abundance of peace.

"And the peace of God that surpasses all understanding will guard your hearts and minds in Christ Jesus"

(Philippians 4:7, NET).

"I have said these things to you, that in me you may have peace. In the world you will have tribulation. But take heart; I have overcome the world"

(John 16:33, ESV).

Scriptural Meditation

Philippians 4:7

Daily Faith Confession

DAY 36

Today, I confess that my son has abundance of joy. He will enjoy joy overflow.

"May the God of hope fill you with all joy and peace in believing, so that by the power of the Holy Spirit you may abound in hope"

(Romans 15:13, ESV).

"For you shall go out in joy and be led forth in peace; the mountains and the hills before you shall break forth into singing, and all the trees of the field shall clap their hands"

(Isaiah 55:12, ESV).

Scriptural Meditation

Romans 15:13, ESV

Daily Faith Confession

DAY 37

Today, I confess that my son has the goodness of God. His life will reflect the character of God.

"Finally, brethren, be joyful, secure perfection of character, take courage, be of one mind, live in peace. And then God who gives love and peace will be with you"

(2 Corinthians 13:11, WNT).

"But as he who called you is holy, you also be holy in all your conduct"

(1 Peter 1:15, ESV).

Scriptural Meditation

1 Peter 1:15, ESV

Daily Faith Confession

DAY 38

Today, I confess that all my son's needs are supplied in glory by Christ Jesus

"And my God will supply your every need according to his glorious riches in Christ Jesus"

(Philippians 4:19, NET).

"Delight yourself in the Lord, and he will give you the desires of your heart"

(Psalm 37:4, ESV).

"A Psalm of David. The Lord is my shepherd; I shall not want"

(Psalm 23:1, ESV).

Scriptural Meditation

Psalm 37:4, ESV

_____
_____
_____
_____
_____
_____
_____
_____
_____
_____
_____
_____
_____
_____
_____
_____
_____
_____
_____
_____

Daily Faith Confession

DAY 39

Today, I confess that my son has overcome every negative situation.

"All things are lawful for me," but not all things are helpful. "All things are lawful for me," but I will not be enslaved by anything"

(1 Corinthians 6:12, ESV).

"And we know that for those who love God all things work together for good, for those who are called according to his purpose"

(Romans 8:28, ESV).

Scriptural Meditation

Romans 8:28, ESV

Daily Faith Confession

DAY 40

Today, I confess that God's divine favour will locate my son.

"I will restore to you the years that the swarming locust has eaten, the hopper, the destroyer, and the cutter, my great army, which I sent among you"

(Joel 2:25, **ESV**).

"For you bless the righteous, O Lord; you cover him with favor as with a shield"

(Psalm 5:12, **ESV**).

Scriptural Meditation

Joel 2:25, ESV

Daily Faith Confession

DAY 41

Today, I confess that the richness of God is for my son to enjoy.

"Blessed be the God and Father of our Lord Jesus Christ, who has blessed us in Christ with every spiritual blessing in the heavenly places"

(Ephesians 1:3, ESV).

"And God is able to make all grace abound to you, so that having all sufficiency in all things at all times, you may abound in every good work"

(2 Corinthians 9:8, ESV).

Scriptural Meditation

2 Corinthians 9:8, ESV

Daily Faith Confession

DAY 42

Today, I confess that my son is translated into the kingdom of God's dear Son.

For he has rescued us from the dominion of darkness and brought us into the kingdom of the Son he loves,

(Colossians 1:13,NIV).

To open their eyes, *and* to turn *them* from darkness to light, and *from* the power of Satan unto God, that they may receive forgiveness of sins, and inheritance among them which are sanctified by faith that is in me.

(Acts 26:18, KJV).

Scriptural Meditation

(Colossians 1:13,NIV).

Daily Faith Confession

DAY 43

Today, I confess that my son is redeemed from the curse of the land.

"Christ redeemed us from the curse of the law by becoming a curse for us—for it is written, "Cursed is everyone who is hanged on a tree"

(Galatians 3:13, ESV).

"Let them curse, but you will bless! They arise and are put to shame, but your servant will be glad!"

(Psalm 109:28, ESV)

Scriptural Meditation

Galatians 3:13, ESV

Daily Faith Confession

DAY 44

Today, I confess that lack has no hold on my son's destiny.

"The young lions suffer want and hunger; but those who seek the Lord lack no good thing"

(Psalm 34:10, ESV).

"A Psalm of David. The Lord is my shepherd; I shall not want"

(Psalm 23:1, ESV).

Scriptural Meditation

Psalm 23:1, ESV

Daily Faith Confession

DAY 45

Today, I confess that my son is delivered from the hand of every strong man holding him down.

"The name of the Lord is a strong tower; the righteous man runs into it and is safe"

(Proverbs 18:10, ESV).

"The fear of man lays a snare, but whoever trusts in the Lord is safe. Many seek the face of a ruler, but it is from the Lord that a man gets justice"

(Proverbs 29:25-26, ESV).

Scriptural Meditation

Proverbs 29:25-26, ESV

Daily Faith Confession

DAY 46

Today, I confess that my son will arise and take his place in destiny.

"Before I formed you in the womb I knew you, and before you were born I consecrated you; I appointed you a prophet to the nations"

(Jeremiah 1:5, ESV).

"And the glory of the Lord shall be revealed, and all flesh shall see it together, for the mouth of the Lord has spoken"

(Isaiah 40:5, ESV).

Scriptural Meditation

Isaiah 40:5, ESV

Daily Faith Confession

DAY 47

Today, I confess that my son will arise and shine his light for the world to see.

"Arise, shine, for your light has come, and the glory of the Lord has risen upon you"

(Isaiah 60:1, **ESV**).

"In the same way, let your light shine before others, so that they may see your good works and give glory to your Father who is in heaven"

(Matthew 5:16, **ESV**).

Scriptural Meditation

Isaiah 60:1, ESV

Daily Faith Confession

DAY 48

Today, I confess that backwardness has no
hold on my son's destiny.

"For those whom he foreknew he also predestined to be conformed to the image of his Son, in order that he might be the firstborn among many brothers"

(Romans 8:29, **ESV**).

"And we know that for those who love God all things work together for good, for those who are called according to his purpose"

(Romans 8:28, **ESV**).

Scriptural Meditation

Romans 8:29, ESV

Daily Faith Confession

DAY 49

Today, I confess that shame has no hold on my son's destiny.

"But the Lord God helps me; therefore I have not been disgraced; therefore I have set my face like a flint, and I know that I shall not be put to shame"

(Isaiah 61:7, **ESV**).

"Instead of your shame there shall be a double portion; instead of dishonor they shall rejoice in their lot; therefore in their land they shall possess a double portion; they shall have everlasting joy"

(Isaiah 50:7, **ESV**).

Scriptural Meditation

Isaiah 50:7, ESV

Daily Faith Confession

DAY 50

Today, I confess that failure has no hold on my son's destiny.

"My flesh and my heart may fail, but God is the strength of my heart and my portion forever"

(Psalm 73:26, ESV).

"I can do all things through him who strengthens me"

(Philippians 4:13, ESV).

Scriptural Meditation

Psalm 73:26, ESV

How to be saved

If you haven't known God personally, here are four principles that will help guide you into a relationship with Him:

1. GOD LOVES YOU AND CREATED YOU TO KNOW HIM PERSONALLY

The most well-known verse in the Bible says, *"God so loved the world, that he gave his only Son, that whoever believes in him should not perish but have eternal life"* (John 3:16, ESV).

You see, this life is not the end of us. This life is preparation for eternity. We have the freedom to decide where we want to spend eternity: with God or apart from Him.

God thinks you're so valuable that He wants to spend eternity with you! The Bible says, *"Now this is eternal life: that they may know you, the only true God, and Jesus Christ, whom you have sent"* (John 17:3).

He planned the universe and orchestrated history, including the details of our lives, so that we could become His friends.

So what prevents us from knowing God personally?

2. MAN IS SINFUL AND SEPARATED FROM GOD, SO WE CANNOT KNOW HIM PERSONALLY OR EXPERIENCE HIS LOVE BECAUSE OF OUR SINS

The Bible says, *"All have sinned and fall short of the glory of God"* (Romans 3:23).

Visualize God in heaven and man on the earth with a great gulf separating the two. Man is continually trying to reach God and establish a personal relationship with Him through his own efforts, such as a good life, philosophy, or religion—but he inevitably fails.

The Bible says, *"The wages of sin is death* [separation from God]*"* (Romans 6:23). The third principle explains the only way to bridge this separation.

3. JESUS CHRIST IS GOD'S ONLY PROVISION FOR MAN'S SIN. THROUGH HIM ALONE CAN WE KNOW GOD PERSONALLY AND EXPERIENCE GOD'S LOVE

JESUS DIED IN OUR PLACE

"God demonstrates his own love for us in this: While we were still sinners, Christ died for us" (Romans 5:8 NIV).

HE ROSE FROM THE DEAD

"Christ died for our sins, just as the Scriptures said. He was buried, and he was raised from the dead on the third day, just as the Scriptures said. He was seen by Peter and then by the Twelve. After that, he was seen by more than 500 of his followers at one time" (1 Corinthians 15:3-6, NLT).

HE IS THE ONLY WAY TO GOD

"Jesus said to him, 'I am the way, and the truth, and the life; no one comes to the Father, but through Me'" (John 14:6, NASB).

Visualize now that God has bridged the gulf that separates us from Him by sending His Son, Jesus Christ to die on the cross in our place to pay the penalty for our sins. Yet, it's not enough just to know these truths.

4. WE MUST INDIVIDUALLY RECEIVE JESUS CHRIST AS SAVIOR AND LORD. THEN WE CAN KNOW GOD PERSONALLY AND EXPERIENCE HIS LOVE.

WE MUST RECEIVE CHRIST

"As many as received him, to them he gave the right to become children of God, even to those who believe in his name" (John 1:12, NASB).

WE RECEIVE CHRIST THROUGH FAITH

"It is by grace you have been saved, through faith-and this not from yourselves, it is the gift of God-not by works, so that no one can boast" (Ephesians 2:8–9, NIV).

WHEN WE RECEIVE CHRIST, WE EXPERIENCE A NEW BIRTH.

The Bible tells of how a man named Nicodemus experienced a new birth through Christ:

There was a man named Nicodemus, a Jewish religious leader who was a Pharisee. After dark one evening, he came to speak with Jesus. "Rabbi," he said, "we all know that God has sent you to teach us. Your miraculous signs are evidence that God is with you." Jesus replied, "I tell you the truth, unless you are born again, you cannot see the Kingdom of God." "What do you mean?" exclaimed Nicodemus. "How can an old man go back into his mother's womb and be born again?" Jesus replied, "I assure you, no one can enter the Kingdom of God without being born of water and the Spirit. Humans can reproduce only human life, but the Holy Spirit gives birth to spiritual life. So don't be surprised when I say, You must be born again. The wind blows wherever it wants. Just as you can hear the wind but can't tell where it comes from or where it is going, so you can't explain how people are born of the Spirit. (John 3:1-8, NLT)

WE RECEIVE CHRIST BY PERSONAL INVITATION

Jesus Christ says, *"Behold, I stand at the door and knock; if anyone hears my voice and opens the door, I will come in to him and dine with him, and he with me"* (Revelation 3:20, NASB).

Receiving Christ involves turning to God from self and trusting Christ to come into our lives to forgive us of our sins and to make us what He wants us to be. Just to agree intellectually that Jesus Christ is the Son of God and that He died on the cross for our sins is not enough. Nor is it enough to have an emotional experience. We receive Jesus Christ by faith as an act of our free will.

HOW YOU CAN RECEIVE CHRIST RIGHT NOW BY FAITH THROUGH PRAYER

Prayer is just talking with God. He knows your heart, so don't worry about getting your words just right. Here is a suggested prayer to guide you:

Lord Jesus, I want to know You personally. Thank You for dying on the cross for my sins.

I open the door of my life and receive You as my Saviour and Lord. Thank You for forgiving me of my sins and giving me eternal life. Take control of my life. Make me the kind of person You want me to be.

Does this prayer express the desire of your heart? If it does, pray this prayer right now, and Christ will come into your life as promised.

Did you pray to receive Christ just now?

If so, congratulations! Luke 15:7 says that when one sinner accepts Jesus Christ as his or her Saviour the angels rejoice. So there's a party going on in heaven right now over your decision! Remember this date as your "second birthday," the day you were born into a new life in Christ! You have God's Word that He answered your prayer.

The Bible promises eternal life to all who receive Christ: *"God has given us eternal life, and this life is in his Son. He who has the Son has the life; he who does not have the Son of God does not have the life. I write these things to you who believe in the name of the Son of God so that you may know that you have eternal life"* (1 John 5:11–13, NIV).

Thank God often that Christ is in your life and He will never leave you (Hebrews 13:5).

You can know on the basis of His promise that Christ lives in you and that you have eternal life from the very moment you invited Him in.

Other books by Dotun Oyewopo

As glorious women, our self-worth should be based on the light of the knowledge God has shone into our hearts through His Word. The Word of God has clearly defined who we are and who we are not, what we are and what we are not.

Many women focus on their outward adornment; they are very concerned about how they look on the outside because that's what people can see. However, the Bible clearly states that your physical beauty is not the most important aspect of who you are. A lot of women place greater value on clothes, shoes, bags, cars, and jewellery than on the Holy Spirit inside them.

Of course, it is easy to boast about the trappings and riches we have, but that is not what God sees as most significant when He looks at us.

The book *The Glorious Woman* is the secret to manifesting the beautiful woman in you, and helps you to know how you can influence your home, marriage, family, children, career, and ministry positively.

The Bible verses and prayer points are to build, guide, and keep you focused.

Arise and shine daughter of God, for the glory of the Lord is risen upon you.

50 Daily Faith Confessions

Words are super powerful, alive, and active. They can inspire or tear down, work for or against you, condemn or set you free, heal or make you sick, get you in or out of trouble or give you life or death. Which will you choose?

Choose life! The *50 Daily Faith Confessions* will feed your mind, soul, and spirit with powerful truths based on Scripture. Each original declaration will help you set a solid foundation in your life. As you boldly speak, obstacles will move, generational curses broken, relationships restored, and your faith increased. You will experience protection, financial prosperity, daily provisions, and God's unmerited favor.

Practicing speaking positively about yourself creates a whole new world around you. It's a sure way to turn your life around as your mind and spirit are saturated and transformed by Scripture. Replace negative self-talk, self-condemnation, fear, and gloom with a narrative of life, faith, joy, and great possibilities. No matter what life throws your way, this powerful collection of faith declarations will empower, equip, and motivate you to overcome and live like a champion.

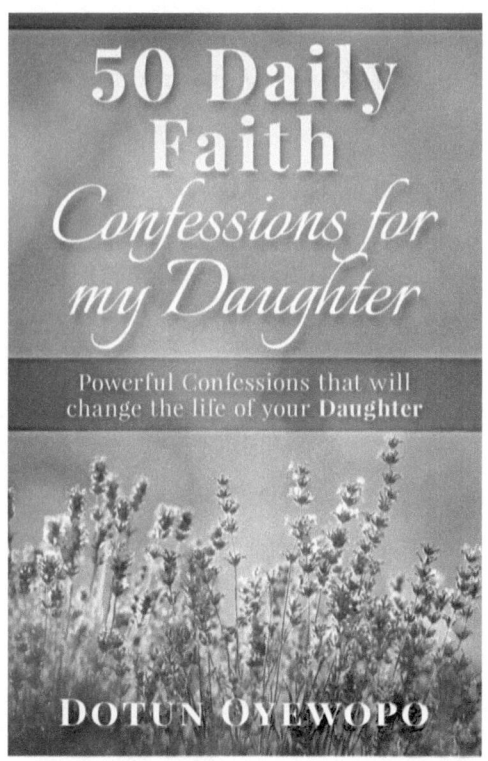

50 Daily Faith Confessions for Your Daughter

Speak life into your daughters with these powerful daily confessions. What you say will make the difference now and in the future. Do you want your daughter to reach her full potential? Do you wish her a life of good health, great relationships, and prosperity? Do you want her to live godly and manifest all the promises of God?

Boldly declare these confessions daily and invoke God's blessings on your daughter. Then watch the remarkable transformation. *Fifty Daily Faith Confessions for My Daughter* is an impactful prayer guide filled with original declarations and Scripture-based prayer points. It is grounded in the Word and helps you to focus on making specific, strategic proclamations.

The world can be a harsh place for girls and women to live. Evil pronouncements—heard and unheard—are made every day over them, some even before birth. This book is a critical tool for every mother and father to break generational and other curses on your daughter's life. Get a copy today and reverse the curses of death, rebellion, low self-esteem, barrenness, failed marriages, negative self-talk, and other ills. As you do so, you will both experience the abundant promises of God in His Word.

You possess what you confess!